SOUTH CAROLINA

by Mary Dykstra

GARETH**STEVENS**
PUBLISHING
A Member of the WRC Media Family of Companies

Please visit our web site at: www.garethstevens.com
For a free color catalog describing Gareth Stevens Publishing's
list of high-quality books and multimedia programs, call
1-800-542-2595 (USA) or 1-800-387-3178 (Canada).
Gareth Stevens Publishing's fax: (414) 332-3567.

Library of Congress Cataloging-in-Publication Data

Dykstra, Mary, 1952–
    South Carolina / Mary Dykstra.
       p. cm. — (Portraits of the states)
    Includes bibliographical references and index.
    ISBN 0-8368-4675-3 (lib. bdg.)
    ISBN 0-8368-4694-X (softcover)
    1. South Carolina—Juvenile literature. I. Title. II. Series.
 F269.3.D94   2006
 975.7—dc22   2005054330

This edition first published in 2006 by
Gareth Stevens Publishing
A Member of the WRC Media Family of Companies
330 West Olive Street, Suite 100
Milwaukee, WI 53212 USA

This edition copyright © 2006 by Gareth Stevens, Inc.

Editorial direction: Mark J. Sachner
Project manager: Jonatha A. Brown
Editor: Catherine Gardner
Art direction and design: Tammy West
Picture research: Diane Laska-Swanke
Production: Jessica Morris and Robert Kraus

Picture credits: Cover, pp. 4, 16, 25 © Gibson Stock Photography; p. 5
© PhotoSpin; pp. 6, 9 © MPI/Getty Images; p. 8 © North Wind Picture
Archives; p. 12 © Hulton Archive/Getty Images; pp. 15, 20, 24 © John Elk III;
p. 17 © Tim Boyle/Getty Images; pp. 21, 22, 26, 28 © Pat & Chuck Blackley;
p. 27 © Graeme Teague; p. 29 © Doug Pensinger/Getty Images

Printed in the United States of America

1 2 3 4 5 6 7 8 9 10 09 08 07 06

CONTENTS

★ ★

Words that are defined in the Glossary appear
in **bold** the first time they are used in the text.

On the Cover: Tourists from around the world enjoy the sand and
surf at Myrtle Beach.

Introduction

South Carolina is not a large state. You can drive from the western border to the Atlantic Ocean in just a few hours. If you care to, you can hike in the Blue Ridge Mountains in the morning. Then, you can head for the coast and lie on a sandy beach in the afternoon. In between, you can visit some of the loveliest cities and towns in the South. You can also stop along the way to see old battlefields and other historic sites.

From its quiet trails to its busy cities, and from the old to the new, this state is brimming with things to see and do. South Carolina is a small state with a great deal to offer!

Hilton Head Island is popular with boaters. Golfers and other tourists also enjoy the island.

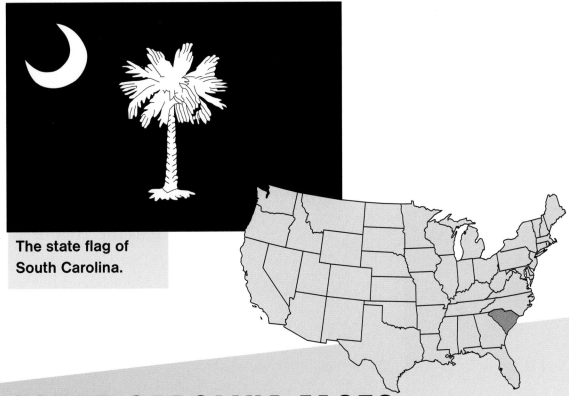

The state flag of
South Carolina.

SOUTH CAROLINA FACTS

- Became the 8th U.S. State: May 23, 1788
- Population (2004): 4,198,068
- Capital: Columbia
- Biggest Cities: Columbia, Charleston, North Charleston, Greenville
- Size: 30,109 square miles (77,982 square kilometers)
- Nickname: The Palmetto State
- State Tree: Palmetto
- State Insect: Carolina mantid (praying mantis)
- State Flower: Yellow jessamine
- State Bird: Carolina wren

History

The first people in South Carolina were Native Americans. They came to this area thousands of years ago. These people lived off the land. They hunted animals and gathered wild plants to eat.

Spanish explorers came to the area in the early 1500s. Their first settlement lasted only a few months. The French also tried to settle here, but they failed as well. In 1566, the Spanish settled on Parris Island. They lived there for more than twenty years. After they left, the British took over the area.

In 1663, the British king gave a large chunk of land to eight of his rich friends. South Carolina was part of this land. One of the men led a group of settlers from

French explorers visited what is now South Carolina in the 1500s.

Name Fame

South Carolina was named after Charles I, who was a British king. He was the father of Charles II. This king granted an area of land, including South Carolina, to eight rich men from Britain.

Britain to this land. They settled at Oyster Point, which is now Charleston.

More settlers from France and England came to South Carolina in the 1680s. Some were traders. They traded with the Natives for furs and then sent the furs back to Europe.

Planters from the island of Barbados also settled in this area. They brought slaves with them. They put the slaves to work growing rice.

As settlers arrived, the Natives suffered. Some were killed in fights with settlers. Others died of diseases that the settlers had.

South Carolina became a **colony** in 1729. The British now held thirteen colonies on the East Coast. In time, the colonists grew tired of being ruled by a king. They wanted to make their own laws. They went to war with the British in 1775. This was the Revolutionary War.

IN SOUTH CAROLINA'S HISTORY

Rice Farming

During the 1840s, nearly half of the rice grown in the United States came from the county of Georgetown in South Carolina. This rice was grown by slaves. At this time, nine out of every ten people in the county were slaves. The slaves had to work very hard. The average slave who worked there lived just nineteen years.

During this war, more battles were fought in South Carolina than in any other colony. In 1780, the British took over Charles Town. Three years later, the colonists forced them out. They renamed the town Charleston. The colonists won the war in 1783. South Carolina became a U.S. state just five years later.

This picture shows the British attacking Fort Moultrie during the Revolutionary War.

Great Divide

In the years after the war, only men who owned land could vote or hold office. Landowners also got part of a vote for each slave they owned. This meant that planters who owned

IN SOUTH CAROLINA'S HISTORY

Trail of Tears

In 1838, thousands of Natives were forced to leave South Carolina. U.S. Army soldiers made them walk all the way to Oklahoma. The trip took four months. Along the way, the weather grew cold, and the Natives had very little food. More than four thousand people died. This terrible journey became known as the Trail of Tears.

land and kept many slaves controlled the state.

By the late 1700s, cotton was being grown in much of South Carolina. It soon became the state's main crop. Much of this cotton was planted, tended, and harvested by slaves who worked on big **plantations**.

In the early 1800s, the U.S. government put a tax on cotton. People in the South thought that the tax was unfair. Vice President John Calhoun of South Carolina was one of them. He argued that states could ignore U.S. laws if they thought the laws were unfair. Calhoun soon became a leader in a fight over **states' rights**.

Cotton Gin

Eli Whitney invented the cotton gin in 1793. The name *gin* is short for "engine." This machine cleans seeds from cotton. Before it was invented, cotton had been cleaned by hand. The cotton gin was much faster. Thanks to this new machine, farmers could grow and sell a lot more cotton.

South Carolina slaves pose for a picture in 1862.

Famous People of South Carolina

Andrew Jackson

Born: March 15, 1767, Waxhaw, South Carolina

Died: June 8, 1845, near Nashville, Tennessee

Andrew Jackson was the first U.S. president to be born in a log cabin. When he grew up, he became a lawyer. Later, he led American troops against the British in the War of 1812. Jackson became a hero during this war, when his men won the Battle of New Orleans. In 1828, he was elected U.S. president. He served two terms.

Northerners and Southerners also argued over slavery. Many people in the North said slavery was wrong. They wanted to pass laws to ban slavery. Planters in the South did not agree. They wanted to keep slaves.

People in South Carolina began to talk about forming their own country. In 1860, South Carolina broke away from the **Union**. Ten more Southern states **seceded** over the next few months. They formed a new country. It was the Confederate States of America.

The Civil War

The North and South began fighting on April 12, 1861. Soldiers from the South shot at Fort Sumter. Soldiers from the North fired back. After two days of fighting, the South won the battle. The Civil War had begun.

Sinker Sub

In 1864, the CSS *H. L. Hunley* became the first submarine ever to sink a warship. It happened off the coast of Charleston. The *Hunley* rammed a Union ship with an explosive on the end of a pole. The blast was so big that both ships sank.

South Carolina suffered badly during the war. The Union army destroyed whole city blocks in Charleston. They set Columbia on fire and wrecked other cities. Many people lost their lives. In all, about one-fourth of the state's soldiers died in the war.

The North won the war in 1865. Then, slavery was banned in the nation. South Carolina joined the Union again three years later. Even so, the Union Army stayed in the state to keep order.

Hard Times

The Army left in 1877. A powerful group of white Southerners took over the state. They did not want African Americans to have the same rights as whites. They passed laws to keep black people from voting. They also made African American children go to their own schools. These schools were never as good as schools for whites. For

IN SOUTH CAROLINA'S HISTORY

The Oldest Senator

In 1996, Strom Thurmond became the oldest U.S. senator in history. He served in the Senate longer than anyone. He was in office for forty-eight years. He retired when he was one hundred years old.

Around 1900, many children worked in the cotton mills of South Carolina.

Around the same time, factories were built in the cities. Most of the factories made cotton cloth. Soon, cloth became the state's top product. People began to move from farms to cities. They found work in the factories.

Equal Rights

many years, life was difficult for black people in this state.

The hard times continued during the early 1900s. A hurricane destroyed rice fields in 1911. This storm brought an end to most of the rice farming in the state. Insects called **boll weevils** ruined the cotton crop in the early 1920s. Many farmers lost their land. Some of them left the state to look for jobs in the North.

In 1954, the conditions for black people began to improve. That year, the U.S. Supreme Court said that both black and white children should attend the same public schools. The white people who were in charge in South Carolina did not agree. They refused to change their schools for nine years. Finally, they gave in. Black and white children now go to the same public schools, and people of all races vote. Everyone has the same rights.

1526	Spanish explorers try to settle in the area of South Carolina and fail.
1663	King Charles II of England gives South Carolina to eight noblemen.
1670	English noblemen lead a group of settlers to South Carolina.
1729	South Carolina becomes a British colony.
1775	The Revolutionary War begins.
1786	Columbia becomes the state capital.
1788	South Carolina approves the U.S. Constitution and becomes a state.
1861	The Civil War begins at Fort Sumter. South Carolina fights for the South during the war.
1868	South Carolina is readmitted to the Union.
1911	A hurricane destroys the state's rice plantations.
1963	Black and white children begin to attend the same public schools.
1989	Hurricane Hugo hits the coast and causes many deaths.
1996	Strom Thurmond sets the record for the most years in the U.S. Senate.

CHAPTER 3

People

More than four million people live in South Carolina. About half of them live in or near cities. The rest live on farms and in small towns. Columbia is the state's largest city.

The People, Then and Now

Native Americans were the first people to live in this area. When Europeans arrived, they killed many Native people. Other Natives died of diseases they caught

Hispanics: In the 2000 U.S. Census, 2.4 percent of the people in South Carolina called themselves Latino or Hispanic. Most of them or their relatives came from places where Spanish is spoken. They may come from different racial backgrounds.

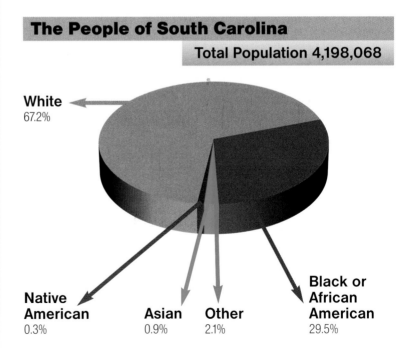

The People of South Carolina

Total Population 4,198,068

White
67.2%

Native American
0.3%

Asian
0.9%

Other
2.1%

Black or African American
29.5%

Percentages are based on the 2000 Census.

Big, beautiful homes line the shore in Charleston. Charleston is the second largest city in South Carolina.

from the settlers. Later, the U.S. Army forced thousands of Natives to leave the state. Very few Native Americans live here today.

Many of the early white settlers came from France and Britain. Others came from Barbados. In later years, people came from Germany and Wales. They were part of a large group of **immigrants** who arrived in the mid-1700s. Today, most of the people in the state were born here. Even so, some people still come to South Carolina from other countries. They come from Mexico, India, and other parts of the world.

In the 1730s, two-thirds of the people who lived in South Carolina were African

A light in the steeple of St. Philips Church was once used to guide ships into the Charleston harbor.

children. The first school for black children opened thirty years later. Even so, public schools were not open in all parts of the state until after the Civil War.

The first college in South Carolina was the College of Charleston. It opened in 1770. Today, the state has more than sixty colleges and universities. The largest of them is the University of South Carolina at Columbia. This university serves more than 25,000 students. The Citadel is a famous military college. It is in Charleston.

Americans. Most of these people were slaves. In the early 1900s, many black people began to leave the state. They moved north and west. They wanted to find good jobs and better lives. Today, about one in three people in this state are African American.

Education

In 1710, laws were passed to provide for schools for poor

Religion

About three out of four people in South Carolina

Jesse Jackson is well known for his powerful speeches. He often speaks up for people in need. He works hard to help others.

are Christian. Most of them belong to Baptist churches. Methodists make up the next largest group. During the 1820s, many Jews lived in Charleston. They founded the first reform Jewish **congregation** in the nation. Today, less than 1 percent of people in the state are Jewish. A small number of Muslims and Buddhists live here, too.

Famous People of South Carolina

Jesse Jackson

Born: October 8, 1941, Greenville, South Carolina

Jesse Jackson has spent many years working for equal rights for African Americans. As a young man, he worked with Dr. Martin Luther King Jr. King was killed in 1968, but Jackson did not give up. He became a Baptist minister and worked for **civil rights**. Jackson also went into politics and ran for U.S. president twice. In 2000, he received the Presidential Medal of Freedom. This award honors people who have done a great deal to help others.

The Land

South Carolina has two main regions. The Up Country in the northwest is mountainous. The Blue Ridge Mountains cover this part of the state. They are part of the Appalachian Mountain range.

Sassafras Mountain is found here. It is the highest point in the state. This peak is 3,560 feet (1,085 meters) above sea level. The Piedmont is east of the mountains. This area is filled with rolling hills.

The southeast two-thirds of the state is called the Low Country. It is part of the Atlantic Coastal Plain. The land is low and flat. The Sea Islands lie offshore. **Salt marshes** and inlets line the coast. The sandy beaches of the Grand Strand also are here. They run along the northern shoreline for more than 60 miles (97 km). Swamps cover much of the land farther from the shore.

Climate

Most of South Carolina is hot and humid. The **Gulf Stream** warms the coastline. It brings warm air inland in winter. The

SOUTH CAROLINA

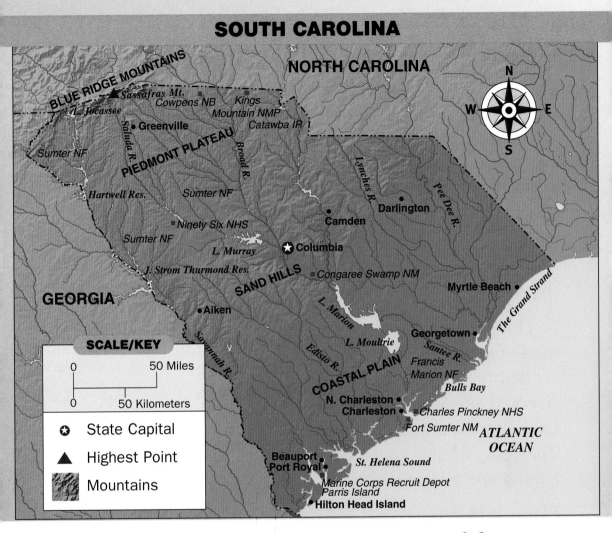

heaviest rains come in late winter and summer. The mountains in the northwest are cooler than the rest of the state.

Hurricanes sometimes hit the state in the summer and fall. These storms bring heavy rain and high winds. Hurricane Hugo did a great deal of damage in 1989. Winds blew up to 138 miles (222 km) per hour along the coast. Near the city of Charleston, the high tide rose 20 feet (6 m)! This tide set a record for the East Coast.

Lakes and rivers

The Savannah River is the longest river in the state. It forms most of South Carolina's western border. Like all of the big rivers in the state, it flows from northwest to southeast. This river empties into the Atlantic Ocean.

This state has several man-made lakes. They were created by building dams on rivers. Lake Moultrie and Lake Marion are the largest. They are popular spots for fishing and boating.

Plants and Animals

South Carolina's plant life is very **diverse**. Near the coast, cypress, magnolia, and live oak trees grow. Spanish moss hangs from tree limbs. Palmettos, with their fan-shaped leaves,

Major Rivers
Savannah River
314 miles (505 km) long
Pee Dee River
233 miles (375 km) long
Edisto River
150 miles (240 km) long

also grow here. Sea oats sprout from the sand dunes. Pine trees grow in flat, sandy areas along the coast. These pine-covered places are called the Pine Barrens.

Cypress trees line the shores of a quiet lake. These trees are common in South Carolina's Low Country.

20

FUN FACTS

All That Glitters

South Carolina is the only state in the East that produces gold. The state is also known for the fine amethysts found in its mines. These purple gemstones are used in jewelry.

In the hilly northwest, loblolly pines are common. Dogwoods and mountain azaleas are found there, too. Forests of oak and hickory are common in the Blue Ridge Mountains.

White-tailed deer live all over the state. This deer is the state mammal. Rabbits, opossums, and beavers are common, too. Alligators live in the state's lakes, swamps, and streams.

Many types of birds live here. Ducks and other birds pass through during spring and fall **migration**. Catbirds, mockingbirds, and ruffed grouse can be seen inland. Warblers and many other small birds also nest here.

The rivers and lakes are home to bluegills, bass, and trout. Clams, shrimp, and other shellfish live in the waters along the coast.

Table Rock Mountain lies in the northwest corner of the state. This area is known as the Up Country.

Economy

Many people in South Carolina work in factories. The top products are cotton cloth and clothing. Chemicals, paper, and rubber products are also made here. Some of these goods are carried to market by ship. The ports of Charleston, Port Royal, and Georgetown are very busy.

Tourism provides many jobs in the state. Workers are needed in hotels, restaurants, and other places tourists go. On Hilton Head Island, more than half of all jobs are related to tourism.

Farms, Forests, and Mines

The top crops in this state are tobacco and soybeans. Peaches and cotton are widely

Boats dock at Port Royal, on South Carolina's coast.

grown, too. Many of the state's farmers raise beef cattle and chickens.

The forests provide wood that is made into paper and lumber. The ocean supports the fishing business. Crabs, shrimp, and oysters are the top ocean products.

South Carolina has about five hundred mines. They yield sand, clay, gravel, and gold. Kaolin is also mined here. This white clay is used to make pottery and medicine. South Carolina leads the country in kaolin mining. It also leads in mica mining.

Several U.S. military posts provide jobs. Many people work at Fort Jackson in Columbia. Others staff the Marine Corps Recruit Depot on Parris Island. Still others work at the Charleston Air Force Base.

How Money Is Made in South Carolina

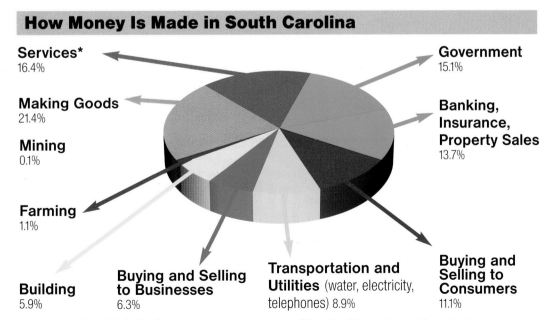

Services*
16.4%

Making Goods
21.4%

Mining
0.1%

Farming
1.1%

Building
5.9%

Buying and Selling to Businesses
6.3%

Transportation and Utilities (water, electricity, telephones) 8.9%

Buying and Selling to Consumers
11.1%

Government
15.1%

Banking, Insurance, Property Sales
13.7%

* Services include jobs in hotels, restaurants, auto repair, medicine, teaching, and entertainment.

CHAPTER
★ ★ ★ ★ ★ ★ ★ ★

6

Government

Columbia is the capital of South Carolina. The leaders of the state work there. The state government has three parts. They are the executive, legislative, and judicial branches.

Executive Branch

The executive branch carries out the state's laws and oversees the budget. The governor is the head of this branch. The lieutenant governor helps the governor. Many other officials also work in this branch.

The state capitol is known as the South Carolina State House.

Legislative Branch

The General Assembly makes laws for the state. This legislative body has two parts. They are the Senate and the House of Representatives.

Judicial Branch

Judges and courts make up the judicial branch. They may decide whether people who have been accused of committing crimes are guilty.

Local Government

South Carolina has forty-six counties. Most are run by a manager and a council.

SOUTH CAROLINA'S STATE GOVERNMENT

Executive		Legislative		Judicial	
Office	**Length of Term**	**Body**	**Length of Term**	**Court**	**Length of Term**
Governor	4 years	Senate (46 members)	4 years	Supreme (5 justices)	10 years
Lieutenant Governor	4 years	House of Representatives (124 members)	2 years	Appeals (9 judges)	6 years

Things to See and Do

Back in Time

Many old plantation houses are open for tours. The tours give visitors a sense of what life was like in the South long ago. Magnolia Plantation in Charleston is a good place to visit. It has gardens and a huge house. Middleton Place is another place to see. It has the oldest formal gardens in the country.

Magnolia Plantation is known for its beautiful grounds and formal gardens.

South Carolina is the place to go for fun in the sun! Many people head straight to Hilton Head Island. It is well known for sandy beaches and great golf courses. Myrtle Beach is a very popular spot, too. Its golf courses and beaches draw huge numbers of tourists.

Visitors enjoy many kinds of water sports in the state. Some of them surf or scuba dive. Others prefer to paddle canoes or kayaks.

The state has many places where visitors can enjoy nature. A favorite spot for nature lovers is Congaree Swamp National Monument. The trees there are some of the tallest in the East. South Carolina also has more than forty state parks. Santee State Park is on Lake Marion. This park offers good fishing and boating. Many parks are found in the Up Country. Hikers who visit Table Rock and Oconee State Parks enjoy wonderful views of the Blue Ridge Mountains.

Places in History

The Charleston Museum is the oldest museum

Fort Sumter is across the bay from Charleston. The first shots of the Civil War were fired there.

Basketmakers display their wares at a market in Charleston. These baskets are woven from a special grass known as sweetgrass.

Fort Sumter National Monument is just a short ferry ride from Charleston. Many people visit the fort to learn about the Civil War.

Each May, the Gullah Festival is held in Beaufort. Gullahs are **descendants** of slaves who lived on the Sea Islands. Most of them came from West Africa. At the festival, artists make baskets called "fanners." Visitors enjoy storytelling, music, and dance.

in the nation. It is a great place to learn about the history of the state. Charleston also is home to the Old Slave Mart Museum. It is in a building where slaves were once sold. Today, it displays African American arts and crafts.

College sports are popular here. Football fans cheer for the University of South Carolina Gamecocks and the

Famous People of South Carolina

Althea Gibson

Born: August 25, 1927, Silver, South Carolina

Died: September 28, 2003, East Orange, New Jersey

Althea Gibson was a great tennis player. She won her first big match when she was fifteen years old. In 1957, she won the women's title at Wimbledon in Britain. She was the first African American woman to win this event. She went on to win the U.S. national title that same year and again in 1958. Later, Gibson became a golfer. She did very well at that sport, too.

Clemson University Tigers. NASCAR auto races attract crowds, too. Racing fans like the Stock Car Hall of Fame at Darlington Raceway. Horse races are held each year in Aiken and Camden.

Touchdown! Reggie Merriweather of the Clemson Tigers scores against the Maryland Terrapins.

29

★ ★

boll weevils — insects that feed on cotton plants

civil rights — the rights of all people to be treated as equals under the law

colony — a group of people living in a new land but being controlled by the place they came from

congregation — a group of people who get together to worship

descendants — children, grandchildren, and other relatives in a family

diverse — different; varied

Gulf Stream — a current of warm water in the Atlantic Ocean that runs along the East Coast

immigrants — people who leave one country to live in another country

meteorite — a chunk of rock from outer space that has landed on Earth

migration — moving from one place to another with the change of season

plantations — large farms where cotton or other crops are grown

salt marshes — flat lands that are often flooded by salt water

seceded — pulled or broke away from

states' rights — the rights of states to make their own laws

tourism — traveling for fun

Union — the United States of America; the Northern states during the Civil War

Books

Andrew Jackson. Getting to Know the U.S. Presidents (series). Mike Venezia (Children's Press)

Civil War Sub: The Mystery of the Hunley. All Aboard Reading (series). Kate Boehm Jerome (Grosset & Dunlap)

Fort Sumter. Cornerstones of Freedom (series). Brendan January (Children's Press)

Jesse Jackson. Journey to Freedom (series). James Meadows (Child's World)

Life on a Plantation. Historic Communities (series). Bobbie Kalman (Crabtree)

Little Muddy Waters: A Gullah Folk Tale. Ronald Daise. (Sandlapper)

South Carolina. Rookie Read-About Geography (series). Janelle Cherrington (Children's Press)

Web Sites

Enchanted Learning: Iowa
www.enchantedlearning.com/usa/states/southcarolina/

Gullah Life
www.knowitall.org/gullahnet/

SC Life: Virtual Nature Field Trips
www.knowitall.org/sclife/

INDEX